for Liz & John
from Marion
with love

Creative Child-Spirit Rescue

Journeys travelled to reunite a life

A fact-based story by

Marion Elmes

British Library Cataloguing-In-Publication Data
A catalogue record of this book is available
from the British Library.

ISBN 978 1 9160531 1 3

Printed and bound in Great Britain
by Print2Demand Ltd, Westoning

Published via pgprintandofficeservices.co.uk

Front cover painting and photographs are by Marion Elmes

This story is dedicated to John

my sounding-board, adviser and supporter
who also helped to re-ignite my love of steam locomotives
which fired this story into life!

Creative Child-Spirit Rescue

Introduction

In 1958 I was an 11+ casualty, resulting in me rejecting my inner day-dreamy creative child spirit – because it was safer that way.

This is a fact-based poem-play. A story of a rejected part of me being left behind on a beach all those years ago – where my creative spirit waits to be rescued and collected to re-unite a life.

The story is based on a beach and is interwoven with waves, dogs, a railway station, mental hospital memories and steam locomotives.

These are powerfully imaginative multi-layered journeys – strands of a child's experiences of failure, rejection, abandonment and not daring to tell, until now …

September 1958

What do you mean, you can't?
There's no such word as can't!

Stop your bleating
Do as you're *told!*

She's failed
She has *failed* the 11+

She's the first in our family to *fail!*

And the family frowned and furied
In our family *no-one* fails
Mother's mutterings strayed from her bedroom
Day and night she stayed there – muttering
Now what? Now what. Now what.

Mother had failed in her family's eyes
all those years ago
and raw memories had jarred her
jerked her back
Now it was happening all over again …

A family's fear of failure passed down and down, on and on

… and behind closed doors Mother was muttering
She can*not* go to that old Secondary Modern –
that *dreadful* school.

So, I got a place at the local Convent –
a lovely school, full of light, on my interview day

… but behind closed doors, Grandma was muttering
No granddaughter of *mine* is going to a Catholic School
Over my dead body.

Mother's mutterings continued …
behind closed doors
She has *got* to go to the High School. She *must* go there.
Must must must mutterings.

Mother demanded of the County Education Officer
that I be given a place at the local High School for Girls

… and suddenly I was told I had 'passed' the 11+
and I *wasn't* going to the Convent
I *was* going to the High School.

I puzzled. I fretted
What *was* going on?
I twisted. I turned
I saw no way out of my mind-whirls
My tummy ached with *BIG* bitter muddy yellow aches.

Every morning before I had to go to the *BIG* school,
in my stomach, terror reared.

Shut down
Refuse to go to school
Safer that way.

I refused.

Children being sick!

No-one asked me *why* I wouldn't go to school …

I was *told* to go
Told to do what I was *told.*

I refused
They'll be *sick* again
Then one day I dared to complain of tummy ache …

Mother marched me off to the Doctor

He didn't ask me what was wrong
She's been complaining of tummy ache, Mother told him
He told her there was nothing physically wrong with me
The Doctor said there's nothing wrong with you
So *now* do as you're told!
And go to school.

I refused
Sick!

Then Mother was put in the local Mental Hospital
madly muttering that she couldn't cope
That I was too much trouble for her
Manic Depression, they said
from behind closed Consulting Room doors.

We would visit her in Hospital on Saturday mornings,
Father and I
We'd all sit on a hard little bench in the Hospital grounds
as Mother muttered on and on … ignoring me.

Father kept insisting – don't tell anyone that your Mother
is in a Mental Hospital
It upsets people.

Left alone at home, a nice neighbour had agreed to feed me
She'll bring you lunch every day
She'll make you special meals that she knows you will like
Father had told me.

But she didn't ask me what I liked
How could she know? I whispered to myself.

And didn't eat
I might be *SICK*.

Then one morning in October the taxi came
Father bundled me into the back, screaming
A little brown suitcase beside me
One hundred miles later,
Father left me, crying …

I can't help it
I don't understand …
Why have you put me in here?
In this Mental Hospital
… *just because I refused to go to school?*

Behind closed doors, our family Doctor
was dead against me being Sectioned
but the 'powers that be' won.

After two months in the Mental Hospital, the Parents came –
one deep dark December day – in the little black Austin car,
to take me home.

It was a sad little drive to see the sea on our way back. I decided
there and then it wasn't safe to have my wild-spirited child
within come home with us. So I left my inner creative
Child-Spirit there on the beach … filleted of love and joy.

* * *

December 1958

I had left my creative Child-Spirit on that beach, below the railway station. It wasn't safe for her to live at home, as part of the family …

Narrator

This weak and floaty little drifter struggles her way towards the station each day and back to the safety of the waves each night.

She knows she must reach the station at the top of this beach where she's been abandoned … and wait and wait and hang on to her tiny scrap of life, watching as every train stops. But no-one comes for her. She's waiting to be found, collected and freed. For years she waits.

* * *

Child-Spirit finds a dog that comes to visit the beach and sinks up to its neck in quick-sands – being buried alive in a liquefying sandpit as the tide comes in. Child-Spirit whines when she finds the dog. Her spirit wills it to escape.

Child-Spirit

    I scream
    STOP!
    It's not free
    Give me more time

It's clawing
It's coming out! I willed harder
The more I hated the sea
Get back brute!
I cry at the black surf behind me
The head yelps
But I'm only trying to help
To save you
Stupid limpet
DO something
You fight for *your* freedom!

Narrator

Sands wash into the dog's hole left as the tide slinks in,
burying the pit in shifting sandy muds. High in the air the dog
had leapt and run away. Trembling, yelping, it was gone.

Child-Spirit

I pawed the air where its shape had left
Come back!
You've left me
You too
I save you
And you run away.

Remembering

*Shan't-won't-can't go to school. Ever again. They'll be
sick again. Those two behind me in Assembly. Their sick
had splashed up onto my heels and socks. My stomach
nearly puked. I refused to go to school ever again.*

*At home I rocked and rocked, back and forth, back and
forth in the old wooden rocking chair by the dead fire.
Day in, day out.*

8

Till one day
he put me in a Mental Hospital.
For two months.
In the Children's Ward.
A hundred miles from home.

Child-Spirit

Lying awash in wavelets
rocking and rolling me over and over
back and forth till early gulls skim across
the waves still full of Creative Spirit lost
Another daybreak and I am station-bound.

Remembering

How he had put my little brown, battered suitcase next to
me on the back seat of the taxi that morning.

Behind my back he'd packed it in the dead of the night
before, with all my bits of clothes and shoes and
toothbrush and said nothing.

"Put your coat on."

"Why?"

"Just do as you're told."

A black taxi had stopped outside our house.

"Go on. Get in."

"Why?"

"You're going away to be made better."

"NO OOOOO!!!"

*Hours later, after being driven over bleak moors, I was
exhausted from screaming in the back seat. "Let me out!
Where are you taking me?"*

*In the back seat Father had to hold me down as I fought,
scratched and bit him. He never said a word that whole
morning. He just silently sobbed as I gave up the fight
and whimpered.*

*The taxi pulled up hours later under a towering building.
Father dragged me out in front of the shut black wooden
doors below a huge clock-face staring down at me.*

*He'd put my little brown battered suitcase on the bottom
of the empty bed that a Nurse had pointed to, next to the
door in a room full of iron bedstead beds, all lined up,
and giggly girls stopped and stared at my bulging red
face.*

*Father had bent over to kiss the top of my head and
without a word, he'd left, crying, silently ...*

Child-Spirit

I creep back down between the posts
Worn sculpted wood laid bare
tongued and holed by seas' smash

Seized jutting rusting bolts scrape my mind
barely-sighted, I feel thread-flayed
catching on splinters
Sun setting blinds, through slits in posts

Lights popping up one by one
as an owl catches its first night-moth
A whistle echoes
Was that the last train of the day?

It had felt like the hundredth and twentieth day
of moving from beach to station and back
to watch and wait

Was it to be today?
Will SHE come for me?
Ever?

Remembering

A new sick feeling rose up one hundred miles from home for reasons I did not understand. HOME-sickness. Even worse than tummy sickness. What have I done wrong? Why am I here? In this crazy Hospital. I am SURE it's all been a BIG mistake...

Narrator

Black shadowy birds, cross-shaped, wheel above and skies fill with their circlings, hanging below contrails crossing sky blues. White streams, straight as arrows. Cloud lines jab and criss-across. The soft, spindling, curling cloud wisps turn canker-yellow and peach. Colours echo Child-Spirit's moods, as fat black crosses silhouette. Cawings rasp from throats of death that their presence declares.

Ravens, ever watchful, ever there – above and scareless, they are too far away to shoo. Too close to ignore their sounds that cling to her heart's near death-beat. They hang, slowly circling with talons and beaks that can dig deep to kill and pick bones clean.

The noonday tide turns and creeps closer, closer to two strollers in picnic mode. Shufflers scuff on sodden sands as waves tickle their toes.

Child-Spirit

I return to the waves from station-watch
Another day lost, empty of the Woman.

Narrator

They sit on deckchairs, carefully unfolded, carried underarm from the station behind the beach.

A lone white-shirted, black-trousered figure kicks at the surf's edge as foam flips and rolls, curls and furls over his feet, and is spent.

Yellowing brown mud suds to foam from driving, breaking waves. So strong as they rush to shore, and beach-spent they drag back shingle that clatters round his ankle bones.

Child-Spirit

I sense a faint roar
of the last train
that's long gone

I look up
at a jet plane streaking high
Its evening dull red trails slice through deep blue
I sense the sound of surf below
the roar of bubbles clashing
that drag me back into the night …
before
I creep up again
and back deep into the station shelter
for tomorrow's watch and wait in dead air.

* * *

I see sand skidding over sand
singing whining whipping
The days of sand follow days of wind
of rains
of seas so huge
drowning again
as years roll in and out of seasons of fogs and frets
sand storms and seas

with mountainous lumps of waves
and
millpond days
glassy-perfect
glitter harsh
sun-caught
head-on dazzle sight

Me shrivelling
never growing
drifting, floating
a no body
a non-person
a nobody
wasted
in watching time
waiting in waves
watching from waiting room
in station
every
day
just
in case.

Remembering

The tigress-girl pacing the Ward, door-to-door, door-to-door, her head filling with burnt-black demons.

Hospital so hot! Heat belched out of fat, glossy radiators. Everywhere.

No heating at home. I missed the pretty patterns the ice made on the glass inside my bedroom window on cold and frosty mornings.

Couldn't breathe in Hospital heat.

Narrator

A dog yowls. Thwack. It barks. Smack. It squeals. Child-Spirit screams out loud unheard. Dog is dragged into the water that laps around its nose. It is pushed in.

"DRINK!" It won't. It's twice kicked. It's thrashed and thumped then thrown into swamping waves.

"DRINK you mutt!" It disappears, flounders in breakers. It yelps with each tug of its head down under water.

"Drink! Do as you're told! You *bitch.*"

It cowers as each new wave disappears it. Near to drowning now, it's dragged out. It flees till leash snaps shut and lashes begin again.

Child-Spirit

I inch forward
unseen
and watch the dog's skid-marks in the sand
softly crinkle and liquefy
smudge and merge into the next foam-beaten suds
With tail between its legs, dog fades away up the beach

Then dog's squealing skid-marks were never there
their ghost images stay in me
marks of terror
unhealed.

Remembering

Walls punched through by voices thin and wailing.

Narrator

Screaming whistles halt Child-Spirit. She sees far white steam puffing from east and west. Round the bay bend, sand-dunes obscure them, then there they are again. The first trains of the day. Arriving together and crossing at her station.

Today she has double chances. She must meet them.

Child-Spirit
> SHE must be here
> This time!

Narrator

Child-Spirit is blasted by steam which blots her view of the station platform. Rushing into the waiting room, she creeps under the slatted wooden benches.

The sun's castings slide over her and stripe up the walls, slithering slowly over an advert –
> VIROL School Children Need It

The deafening bark of engines announce they are arriving at the station before halting at platform ends. Their barks echo round the station buildings and in under the roof of the open-fronted shelter full of holiday-makers' luggage trolleys and hard, wooden seats, where she waits.

Doors bang. People rush off and on carriages. Child-Spirit stares into the backs of them making for the level crossing gate. Barriers are down. Shutting out all cars and lorries, and a bus queuing – people sitting waiting to leave – because they can. Soon.

Some days are filled with suitcases – little battered brown ones and chunks of sea chests piled high on trolleys ready to load for passengers milling around her invisible being.

On the platform a dog senses her presence and looks up at her. Shivering, it jumps away, ribs gnawing at its belly-skin stretched tight, tail between its legs. Its eye-whites flare. It stops, looks again then sniffing the air around her, its nose reaches out. It pulls back in jerks. It very slowly stretches forward again, then it sniffs and wags its wisp of a tail once, then another wag once to the left then once to the right and stop. Dead centre, it pulls its tail between its legs as its owner jerks it away.

"Heel you stupid mutt! There's nothing there!"

Child-Spirit

    I crouch as spat word-sounds cut
    as dog's last look back mourns
    and with a yelp it's pulled away as engine cylinder cocks
    hiss
    Dog disappears in clouds of steam
    It tries to jump away, whimpering, trembling
    Owner pulls and shouts
    Dog's dragged along on its haunches
    head strangled
    straining to look back
    then, swallowed by steam
    it's gone
    with sharp words flying round its hobbling body
    flinching with every beating
    I cower with each body blow
    I scream at its crippledness
    A near ghost of a dog mirrors the ghost of me.

Narrator

The night nearly never ends as she aches for the dog with its spirit no more. It left the dog's body long ago. Broken way back in puppyhood when habits became ingrained as its owner's private furies were taken out on its tiny body, aching to do what's right. To please at all times. Needing to belong. So desperate to please.

* * *

Narrator

Today she watches a train pull into the station from the east, and from the west a Black Five engine pulling its train halts under the footbridge. Suddenly it blows off its excess steam which streams back and forth in billowing swirls and swamps its engine, half the station, and all passengers disappear.

For a moment they cease to exist. Was The Woman there? Under clouds of steaminess?

Child-Spirit

> Ah, but did SHE come
> Did I miss HER?

Narrator

The whistles blow and the two smoking, steaming chimneys explode with slow, sharp barks as each train pulls away in opposite directions, leaving shadow-casts climbing up the platform walls. And they're gone and all is still.

Two chances for Her to come, but lost. They've both gone without bringing the Woman.

Child-Spirit

> I ache into the waves
> long into each night
> after the Woman does not come.

Narrator

Partying people on the beach scare her. She cowers in waves and watches, hearing squeals through sparking bonfire flames. Couples in shadowy clinches kiss-roll in sands as her waves wash around them. They skinny-dip, splash out and sleep on soft sand.

Child-Spirit crawls by bodies entwined in dawn's clarity. Each other is hugged for body warmth she's never known. Moans, groans, they dress and leave. Scrambling up the beach and rattling across the shingle bank, they stagger on pebbles and slip-slide up to trains arriving to take them home.
Parcels of food, left-over shoes, smashed bottles strewn. Green glass glitters in first light that cuts to the quick.

In six hourly cycles, charred logs roll alongside her. Plastic bottles too. Bags that balloon and swallow fishes and crabs scuttling seaward. Bags that smother-wrap her and suffocate. Crabs claw, fishes nip, flounders flap away into clouds of sand.

Storm-wild waves beat, and peace comes after, with nothingness.

Birds, gannets, cormorants greet with dives. Shelducks circle her, searching daily for mud flats. Scooping with busy red bills, they forage.

They waddle and wade through surf's foaming edges. Hanging around waiting for their favourite mud patches to uncover as the tide falls. They are haughty in their struts. Their stark-white, rust-patched bodies duck-dive out of sight with emerald green flashing through their black heads catching the light. Every year they pair and part.

Remembering

> *Each week the Psychiatrist had told me, "You're not going home this week."*

> *... behind closed doors, he'd diagnosed my Acute Anxiety and had been informed that Mother was not yet ready to have me home.*

> *No. Not ready. NO!*

Searching through muds fresh out of waves, their mirror images move along below them. The shelducks. Gathered together they work, unseeing, unsensing, unhearing Child-Spirit's pleas, screamed into winds dying as she moves through twice-daily tidal dumps of seaweeds storm-torn off by their roots.

Green-brown, bleaching bladderwracks and sea lettuce ripped off and washed up to die. Storm-damaged pulped pickings for birds and tiny crabby creatures in their habitat clinging to fronds – grabbed at, unchewed, swallowed into warm moiling stomachs of gulls. She crawls up through desiccated seaweeds to meet the first train.

Short-haired ginger scruff with stump tail rolls in mud then kicks it high over its back. It slides its muzzle deep through ooze and out again, snorts, sniffs and rolls and its coat turns to milk chocolate mud. It tumbles back upright, shakes, turns and gaining ground, gallops away after its owner.

Child-Spirit

    Is SHE there today
    Will SHE come for me today
    Will this be the one
    The special train that brings HER to collect me?

Narrator

Shelducks fly low, their wing-tips skim the water surface. Child-Spirit senses the air drafts past her and watches the birds skid into sloppy muds and start their red bill shovellings, to be gone by the morning's half tide.

The sea is yellow today. Mud-yellowed. A dull ache yellow. It was striped green-purple yesterday under shadow-casts of cloud bands.

When mid-blue meets the horizon haze, that's when the families come. All through the mid to high-blues of summers they stay.

Indigo March storms are the violent ones when nobody comes. When waves hiss and drag on the shingle shore.

Purple pinks burn deep into orange as mid-year suns disappear behind towering cloud banks.

Tomorrow will be flat grey, she knows, staring up at cloud bubbles. Lace white foam froth appears clear and clean, in days like tomorrow.

Child-Spirit

Trying to move through the holes that form
latticework-like in wave froth
that flattens and fizzes down sandworm holes
and sandworm casts begin to melt
Escaping through foam holes may be my way
to freedom some days
Days when trains don't run
Days when hope fades to foam
Nights when the moon casts shadows on waves,
rearing behind me
Fearful of forces flattening me, smashing me
onto the sand, pebbles and rock bottom

A dog howls.

Narrator

One summer's night Child-Spirit strikes out across to light-shines. Flashings in the far distance. A cluttered clutch of life-saving twinkles, on far shores she's seen from the station on clear, clean nights.

Maybe the Woman will be out there …

20

Child-Spirit is rolled around mid-channel, below heaving overnight ferries. Their passing bow-wave backwashes swamp her. Lovers at rails not seeing her waving, and her crying mind-sores.

Giving up, the tide carries her back. Back to below the station. Back to her beach, her sand, her seaweeds, her foam, her waves, her bed-rock.

Child-Spirit

> I am at the edge. Edge of land. Edge of steam
> Within whistle-shot
> just in case
> one day
> the Woman will come
>
> I count. One flash, two flashes, three flashes, black
> One flash. Black
> Into the dark it sends its numbered messages
> all night every night when I turn away from station lights
> and look North
>
> I know not why I sense that only that light-beat repeat
> is safe
> Is a saver. Mine alone?
> Every night of my waiting, watching, wanting years
> it's there, out there behind me, but too many wave-crests
> away
>
> But, now I know it's a light-beat to save other souls,
> not mine.

Narrator

No wave is the same. No repeats of shape, size, position. Each alone in their togetherness, controlled by forces unseen, unheard, watched but never biddable. Years of seasons piling into seasons. The flows come and go, year upon ten, fold up, unfold, wash out and back, around her daily journey up to the station and back for the first to last train.

Waited. Watched for …

Remembering

> *Night screams. Self-punching thuds I heard. I watched.*
> *Nurses held her down. A needle's jabbed in. A Nurse sat*
> *and stroked her head, to sleep.*

> *They'd given the cops the run-around, that Nadine and*
> *Claudia. They'd escaped from our Children's Ward. The*
> *Police were called. The girls stalked the cops round and*
> *round the Hospital grounds …*

Child-Spirit

> Is SHE to come today
> Why this one
> above all others
> Why not
> Maybe …

Remembering

> *I'll come and see you again next week*
> *come and see you next week*
> *come and see you …*

> *One-two-buckle-my-shoe-one-two-buckle-my-shoe*
> *I growled into bedclothes every Wednesday night*
> *after he'd left me there, crying again.*

Narrator

Emptied of life-juices but still her will threads on through her spirit-body. Today her soul bleeds no more. Dried and sored. Quiet. The death hush of glassy millpond days.

No waves to carry her in, roll around her, cocoon and curl her up.

Dish-flat days, stripped-naked days, barren flats to the far line, hazed up. Occasional cat's paws skitter and scratch the surface in brief breezes and claw.

On days like these.

Remembering

    Madly drawing horses galloping away – on paper with pencils Nurses had given me. Sitting up in bed, propping paper on curled-up knees, hunched over, trying hard not to hear, or look. Galloping away-away.

Narrator

Station flowers in season tell her the time of year. Daffodil yellows dazzle in terracotta pots. Primroses buried in tubs, barely showing above the wooden rims. Pansies later and roses scale to heights beyond her reach.

High tides – springs – bring death-rattles of shingle pebbles dragged in backwashes that haunt her. Reminding her of never-endings. Mud picked up, silt saturates turning waves into milky, frothy coffee frills.

Soot smoke drifts over. Locomotives' fallout smothers gulls when the blow is a south-westerly. Then white steam billows, curls, chases soot-black wisps that melt above her as she tries to catch their tendrils chasing low over the sea's surface.

On golden, quiet, lazy, wave-curl-furl-topple, sunrise ripening days, Child-Spirit soars with gulls gliding on thermals.

Child-Spirit

    Today's the day!
    I know it.

Narrator

This time last year, morning mists glowed into gold and greys and all that happened was that families swarmed down from trains through clouds of steam.

Children shrieked and whooped, swinging buckets and spades. Sunshades and picnic wicker baskets humped over the bumpy pebble ridge to sandy patches just above the mud-line.

"Don't run in the mud! You'll slip. You'll stick. You'll sink. You'll drown!"

Furious furrow-browed grown-ups shouted, running after excitables scattering, as arms are grabbed, legs are smacked and cherub bodies yanked back to base-camps.

Safe and sound, bound and gagged, cherubs sour. They sulk and whine. Whimper and grizzle. Their spirits quashed. They are fed lukewarm squash and curly crusted bloater fish paste sandwiches that gulls surround, cackle and grab at, just out of swipe range.

A dog strays from its family 'pack'. Trots across. Sleek, pot-bellied, pop-eyed, blunt-nosed and black. Its eyes slit as it sniffs around Child-Spirit. Snarling teeth gleam white. The bitch yaps and is called back to within her family bounds. Dog runs back so obediently for scolds and pats.

Child-Spirit

> Free and far from family ties
> bounds and welts, hugs and kisses
> I still yearn to return with HER.

Narrator

Golden mists turn to blinding noonday crackling light and then they're gone. Families swarming up to meet the last trains east and west, pack onto carriages and flop into seats with chuff puff sighs. With sandy toes and sunburnt noses, children curl up and sleep in mothers' laps and Child-Spirit watches from a station bench as engines chuff away and fade to silence.

Another day done. Child-Spirit's signal to crawl down to her wave-bed, sink beneath surface waters and rest and weep to sleep. The Woman didn't come …

Child-Spirit

Shadows fly over, flapping shapes cloud my nights
Morning mirror reflections in glassy seas beyond me
Gulls rest
I sense no shadow of my own
No reflection of my self
I know I don't exist in form or shape

I am a non shape
A nobody
A no body
A no-one

Without the host body of the Woman
I don't exist.

Narrator

A silk-soft sheen lays on greyed silver mud flats. A fish breaks the surface. Leaps through its hoops of rippling water. A cormorant in black-green, silver-wet feathers, dives. Surface skin seals over. Child-Spirit waits for the bird and watches the water as it glasses to stillness. Moments pass … bird pops up and is making circles of tiny waves again.

Child-Spirit

It's one of those silent windless surface days
A sideless, topless, seamless, bottomless day
Just tidal
The long slow creep

out and back
in repeat
that never waits for me.

Narrator

Emptiness splits as a yapping Jack Russell barrels by, chasing the stone thrown into the sea. A stone that's never retrieved by dog hunting until called off. Lost at sea. Back out in splashing sunlight sprays. Its spotlit body patched white and ginger blazes behind its flapping ears, as tail thwacks flanks in semi-circles, flashing back and forth.

Child-Spirit

I love happiness
all bundled up inside
such a little body
galloping free.

Remembering

Woman in Hospital losing her fight with straitjacket.

Child-Spirit

Unbroken waves roll in
like liquid corrugated paper and crinkling silks
Some waves flash silver-centred
They curl or spill
rush up
and death-rattle down the shingle shore into silence

Waves that …

crease, crinkle
curl
crash
chatter
cease

crease, crinkle
curl
crash
chatter
cease

burnt chocolate colour this evening
in unrepeatable repeats

no let up of Nature's forces
waves tick
to earth moon and ocean clocks
as I watch …

* * *

Winds get up in the night
I gulp and gasp in the gale
Grab at the winds that whip over the sands
As I hang on for my dear little life.

Remembering

> *Hospital panics when the winds came. Brain-blown.*

> *Fear, fun and wild excitement ran high when the storms
> hit – when the winds wound us up.*

Child-Spirit

> I soar again as steam screams sky high
> Clouds blast shadow-cast drifts over me
> I sob inside and turn away
> not daring to look at yet another empty platform
> fading into such stern silence.

Narrator

The train sings its sizzling, steaming, hissy wuffy-chuffy songs. Whistling to whoever will be listening out for it. However quiet the engines are kept, unfed with coal, while waiting, they sing.

Then suddenly high into the sky excess steam screams. Cylinder cocks hiss steam, biting at ankles. Kids shriek and squeal, shrinking back into parental folds.

"Don't go near the edge, Tommy!"

Bells ring. Hearts beat fast for next train coming. The crossing gates clank and rattle shut. The red and white signal arm drops and clunks. The approaching loco's whistle and barks bounce off buildings.

"Train's coming!" a child whispers in awe, eyes saucer-wide craning over the platform's edge.

"Get *back*, Tommy. Do as you're *told!*"

The great green-sheened 'Eddystone' Bullied Light Pacific locomotive slows. Its steam blasts over platforms as it halts, pulsing, hissing, spitting, then quiets, just leaking steam gently, throbbing with engine's life-force. Smuts fly, some hot.

It whistles. It barks and the great green locomotive's off again, moving through its massive hissings into a rhythmic momentum – dee-clunk-dee-clunk-dee-clunk – and it's gone.

Sounds bound around green fielded hills and no one is left behind.

* * *

Narrator

The geese arrived today. All the way from the North. To over-winter. Families of them. Landing on wet sands they honk to each other. Exhausted.

* * *

The Woman

They came to collect me from the Hospital one day in the depths of December 1958 – my Parents. The little sit-up-and-beg black Austin bumped over the railway crossing and parked above the beach. We went for a little walk, along the beach, the three of us, not yet together.

But my day-dreamy, creative Child-Spirit wasn't safe to come home with us. Too excitable. Too unpredictable. Too imaginative. So I left her there, on that beach that day. And was driven away without her. It was safer that way.

Remembering

> *Boy crawling across the canteen floor and crouching in a corner, rocking.*

The Woman

We had walked, straggled along the mud-flatted, bleak bare beach. So boring with little flappy waves, curling, plopping. No crash, no force. No life. No fight. Just flop, plop, flop.

I chose to leave her here. On this empty beach, till it would be safe to collect her. When? Who knows when? Not me. How could I? Then, when I was eleven. Too young to know. Too young to cope alone.

When grown-ups couldn't cope with my life-force spirit, how could I?

30

So I left her there, that icy dark day, in mid December and walked back to the little black Austin's back seat and was driven away over the railway lines with not a single look back, neither up nor down the track through crossing gates shut, across the track that ran along the back of the beach.

Remembering

Nobody had asked me why I wouldn't go to school.
Nobody asked me what was wrong.
Nobody asked me what I was feeling and thinking.
Nobody told me I was to be taken to and left
in a Mental Hospital.
Nobody told me why ...
WHY not?

"Respect your Elders and Betters."

"Children should be seen and not heard."

"Grown-ups know what's best for you."

"DON'T answer back!"

"Who do you think you are!"

And "Give me three good reasons why you say you can't. There's no such word as can't."

The Woman

The trains, they would see her. They would look out for her, when they ran in summer, carrying families to the beach.

Collect her? Maybe never. Maybe safer that way.

I shut her out and painted between the lines. Never daring to break out again, to break free and go over the edges. Without permission. Not at home. Never in public.

And I did my sums. And cleaned my shoes. Pulled up my socks. Did as I was told and never answered back. Continued to be seen and not heard, nor listened to. And I smiled shyly at grown-ups, and said, "How do you do," in all the right places and, "I am very well thank you." At all times. It was safer that way.

… and it was safer in arguments, when airing my opinions, to believe that everyone was right and I must be wrong, just in case *they* would have me put back in a Mental Hospital if I dared to disagree with anyone, ever again.

Think …
Don't argue!
They're always right!
It's safer that way.

I was pleased and proud of that clever thought that popped in weeks after I'd left the Hospital …

… and I told no-one why I had missed my first term at the High School.

Father had insisted – don't tell anyone where you've been. It upsets them.

And underground I went, subversively, with those who dared to be free, publicly.

How did they dare, I wondered, in awe and fear. What if I got 'found out'? What if I got attacked for being me? Never daring to be the whole real me.

So, I lived through others who dared. I was their satellite, circling them. Forever looking up from below my parapet, up to them, up there on their pedestals. It was safer that way.

On the surface 'I must be a *nice* girl at all times'.
I never dared paint over the lines or fall off the edges. The me who drowned the rejected creative piece of me – the part of me needing to be found and mended … to find my own track.

And from way beneath the parapet …

I worked hard
Played hard and hurt
Furied hard
Laughed hard and wept.

Always sensing there was something missing
I was forever out of balance
until my Parent 'Controllers' died one by one.

We were all victims and survivors, in our own separate ways.

A Gift for Mother

Below your bedroom window
your late sister's rose
had blazed with thirty blooms
all summer long.

Above the bedded gift
by moth-light you ceased
somewhere in the dead of the night
in that long hot summer gone.

For Father

The tide turned as Father died …
Now he is free of flotsam
that clung on
till his heart bled
and his bilges burst
dumping heavily
all at sea

He's safe now.

The pain, the loss, the grief was great, so I learnt hard and slow, aged forty plus.

'Re-parent your Inner Child,' Therapists had suggested …

Then followed therapies, counselling, self-help books and finally acceptance and forgiveness, now all packed into my Trauma Survivor's Kitbag.

February 2010

The Woman

Then three weeks after his funeral, it was as though the spirit of my father 'sent' me a steam train to drive.

It was a small locomotive to drive for four and a half miles. That's all it took. That's how far away my Child-Spirit was. That's all that stood between me and collecting my creative Child-Spirit from where I'd left her, all those years ago.

Four and a half blessed miles of track. Straight as the gull flies, to the station above the beach where I'd left her. To the station she'd moved to every day since.

She'd waited
Looking out for me
Year on year …

* * *

Narrator

One snow-threatened wind-bitten February afternoon stiff with sleet that spits and hits Child-Spirit, she is shining. She knows it is to be today. Her heart spirit beats.
She KNOWS it is today. She *WILL* come.

A whistle sounds and drifts. Is the Woman coming today?

Child-Spirit's silent scream catches in the wind.
It echoes the whistle bleat way down the line.
The thousandth or more train trundles towards the gates clanking shut across the road.
The loco's here, now, chuffing into the station.
The Woman soars above the engine's heat, flying in with it.

The Woman

Child-Spirit! Child-Spirit?

Child-Spirit

    I hear my name!
    The Woman's not seen me!
    SHE's driving her train on!
    SHE's disappearing!

    … and later, the waves pull me back under.

The Woman

My Child-Spirit had waited and watched, and I didn't know. I'd shut her out. Drowned her out, till that February … three weeks after his funeral, when my father had 'sent' the engine, to try to help, to try to make it right. He who had me Sectioned, all those years ago.

Now, I am aboard the footplate of this little explosive loco, now pulling up the regulator. Then tugging on the whistle chain as we approach the station and braking oh so gently to a halt, suddenly I sense her here.

I know it's time. I am ready now. It's safe. At last I can dare to be me. Now they have gone to beyond the grave. Now I can collect her. My Child-Spirit.

But I *missed* her! At the station. I looked out and she wasn't there!

Did I look the wrong way? She WAS there, I know!

Narrator

Child-Spirit is pulled back to the waves. The lights dim in ghosts of steam-hang and the last to leave the station is the Signalman walking away each night, locking doors and gates as he goes, leaving only an empty platform.

September 2010

The Woman

Then, it was as though he 'sent' me another engine. A big green locomotive. Almost too big for the track. Almost too big for me to handle. Such power, as I drove that loco into the station – her station – and standing idle waiting for permission to leave, my huge loco blasts off her excess steam with a roaring, high into the sky, as if announcing to the world – I AM HERE!

Where are you Child-Spirit? I've come for you!

Narrator

Summer months gone and one September morning a great green steaming Bullied Light Pacific locomotive pulls into Child-Spirit's station. Its fat-bellied boiler blows its top with a scream, blasting a plume of steam high into the sky.

Child-Spirit
 Yes! SHE's up there!
 Coming to rescue me

 I see HER!
 On the footplate

In the cab
SHE's here!

I scream inside, Wait for me. *Please* take me home with you, this time!

Narrator

The Woman's giant engine blows its top, again – announcing to the world that Child-Spirit has been found!

The Woman

I scoop up my Child-Spirit from the platform into the cab, aboard the giant loco's footplate. I hold on oh so tightly and slowly I pull on the great engine's regulator. We are moving. Pulling away with such slow power.

We creep past carriages stuck beside us, behind their stationary steam engine, waiting patiently for us to leave the station.

We look down on holiday families going home. Sitting by carriage windows, they're looking up, waving and smiling at us, waiting for us to leave, to clear the single track for their train to leave.

We watch, and from within one carriage window below us, a mother mouths, "It's a Woman driver!"

Sitting in her lap is a child in a cherry-red dress looking up at us.

The child's eyes are shining –
under her golden curls she is laughing.

She throws up her arms. Her hands stretch out. Her fingers clench. Suddenly she gives us the thumbs-up as we pass!

… and we *too* are going home together

At last!

Marion aged 5

Back cover photograph by John Arney is of Marion aged 64